The Jester's Sword
How Aldebaran, the King's Son Wore the Sheathed Sword of Conquest

Annie F. Johnston

Alpha Editions

This edition published in 2022

ISBN: 9789356318403

Design and Setting By

Alpha Editions

www.alphaedis.com

Email - info@alphaedis.com

As per information held with us this book is in Public Domain.
This book is a reproduction of an important historical work.
Alpha Editions uses the best technology to reproduce historical work
in the same manner it was first published to preserve its original nature.
Any marks or number seen are left intentionally to preserve.

The Jester's Sword

BECAUSE he was born in Mars' month, which is ruled by that red war-god, they gave him the name of a red star—Aldebaran; the red star that is the eye of Taurus. And because he was born in Mars' month, the bloodstone became his signet, sure token that undaunted courage would be the jewel of his soul.

Now all his brothers were as stalwart and as straight of limb as he, and each one's horoscope held signs foretelling valorous deeds. But Aldebaran's so far out-blazed them all, with comet's trail and planets in most favourable conjunction, that from his first year it was known the Sword of Conquest should be his. This sword had passed from sire to son all down a line of kings. Not to the oldest one always, as did the throne, though now and then the lot fell so, but to the one to whom the signs all pointed as being worthiest to wield it.

So from the cradle it was destined for Aldebaran, and from the cradle it was his greatest teacher. His old nurse fed him with such tales of it, that even in his play the thought of such an heritage urged him to greater ventures than his mates dared take. Many a night he knelt beside his casement, gazing through the darkness at the red eye of Taurus, whispering to himself the words the old astrologers had written, "*As Aldebaran the star shines in the heavens, Aldebaran the man shall shine among his fellows.*"

Day after day the great ambition grew within him, bone of his bone and strength of his sinew, until it was as much a part of him as the strong heart beating in his breast. But only to one did he give voice to it, to the maiden Vesta, who had always shared his play. Now it chanced that she, too, bore the name of a star, and when he told her what the astrologers had written, she repeated the words of her own destiny:

"As Vesta the star keeps watch in the heavens above the hearths of mortals, so Vesta the maiden shall keep eternal vigil beside the heart of him who of all men is the bravest."

When Aldebaran heard that he swore by the bloodstone on his finger that when the time was ripe for him to wield the sword he would show the world a far greater courage than it had ever known before. And Vesta smiling, promised by that same token to keep vigil by one fire only, the fire that she had kindled in his heart.

One by one his elder brothers grew up and went out into the world to win their fortunes, and like a restless steed that frets against the rein, impatient to be off, he chafed against delay and longed to follow. For now the ambition that had grown with his growth had come to be more than bone of his bone and strength of his sinew. It was an all-consuming desire which coursed through him even as his heart's blood; for with the years had come an added reason for the keeping of his youthful vow. Only in that way could Vesta's destiny be linked with his.

When the great day came at last for the Sword to be put into his hands, with a blare of trumpets the castle gates flew open, and a long procession of nobles filed through. To the sound of cheers and ringing of bells, Aldebaran fared forth on his quest. The old king, his father, stepped down in the morning sun, and with bared head Aldebaran knelt to receive his blessing. With his hand on the Sword he swore that he would not come home again, until he had made a braver conquest than had ever been made with it before, and by the bloodstone on his finger the old king knew that Aldebaran would fail not in the keeping of that oath.

With the godspeed of the villagers ringing in his ears, he rode away. Only once he paused to look back, when a white hand fluttered at a casement, and Vesta's sorrowful face shone down on him like a star. Then she, too, saw the bloodstone on his finger as he waved her a farewell, and she, too, knew by that token he would fail not in the keeping of his oath.

'Twas passing wonderful how soon Aldebaran began to taste the sweets of great achievement. His name was on the tongue of every troubadour, his deeds in every minstrel's song. And though he travelled far to alien lands, scarce known by hearsay even to the folk at home, his fame was carried back, far over seas again, and in his father's court his name was spoken daily in proud tones, as they recounted all his honours.

Young, strong, with the impetuous blood begotten of success tingling through all his veins, he had no thought that dire mishap could seize on *him;* that pain or malady or mortal weakness could pierce *his* armour, which youth and health had girt about him. From place to place he went, wherever there was need of some brave champion to espouse a weak ones cause. It mattered not who was arrayed against him, whether a tyrant king, a dragon breathing fire, or some hideous scaly monster that preyed upon the villages. His Sword of Conquest was unsheathed for each; and as his courage grew with every added victory, he thirsted for some greater foe to vanquish, remembering his youthful vow.

And as he journeyed on he pictured often to himself the day of his returning, the day on which his vow should find fulfilment. How wide the gates would be thrown open for his welcome! How loud would swell the cheers of those who thronged to do him honour! His dreams were always of that triumphal entrance, and of Vesta's approving smile. Never once the shadow of a thought stole through his mind that it might be far otherwise. Was not he born for conquest? Did not the very stars foretell success?

One night, belated in a mountain pass, he sought the shelter of a shelving rock, and with his mantle wrapped about him lay down to sleep. Upon the morrow he would sally forth and beard the Province Terror in his stronghold; would challenge him to combat, and after long and glorious battle would rid the country of its dreaded foe. Already tasting victory, he fell asleep, a smile upon his lips.

But in the night a storm swept down the mountain pass with sudden fury, uprooting trees a century old, and rending mighty rocks with sword thrusts of its lightning. And when it passed Aldebaran lay prone upon the earth borne down by rocks and fallen trees. Lay as if dead until two passing goat-herds found him and bore him down in pity to their hut.

Long weeks went by before the fever craze and pains began to leave him, and when at last he crawled out in the sun, he found himself a poor misshapen thing, all maimed and marred, with twisted back and face all drawn awry and foot that dragged. One hand hung nerveless by his side. Never more would it be strong enough to use the Sword. He could not even draw it from its scabbard.

As in a daze he looked upon himself, thinking some hideous nightmare had him in its hold. "That is not *I!*" he cried, in horror at the thought. Then as the truth began to pierce his soul, he sat with starting eyes and lips that gibbered in cold fear, the while they still persisted in their fierce denial. "This is not *I!*"

Again he said it and again as if his frenzied words could work a miracle and make him as he was before. Then when the sickening sense of his calamity swept over him like a flood in all its fulness, he cast himself upon the earth and prayed to die. Despair had seized him. But Death comes not at such a call; kind Death, who waits that one may have a chance to rise again and grapple with the foe that downed him, and conquering, wipe the stigma coward from his soul.

So with Aldebaran. At first it seemed that he could not endure to face the round of useless days now stretching out before him. An eagle, broken winged and drooping in a cage, he sat within the goat-herd's hut and gloomed upon his lot, and cursed the vital force within that would not let him die.

To fall asleep with all the world within one's grasp and waken empty-handed—that is small bane to one who may spring up again, and by sheer might wrest all his treasures back from Fortune. But to wake helpless as well as empty-handed, the strength for ever gone from arms that were invincible; to crawl, a poor crushed worm, the mark for all men's pity, where one had thought to win the meed of all men's praise, ah, then to live is agony! Each breath becomes a venomed adder's sting.

Most of all Aldebaran thought of Vesta. The stroke that marred his comeliness and took his strength had robbed him of all power to win his happiness. It was written "by the hearth of him who is the bravest she shall keep eternal vigil." As yet he had not risen above the level of his forbears' bravery, only up to it. Now 'twas impossible to show the world a greater courage, shorn as he was of strength. And even had her horoscope willed otherwise, and she should come to him all filled with maiden pity to share his ruined hearth, he could not say her yea. His man's pride rose up in him, rebellious at the thought of pity from one in whose sight he fain would be all that is strong and comely. Looking down upon his twisted limbs, the pain that racked him was greater torture than mere flesh can feel. Although 'twas casting heaven from him, he drew his mantle closer, hiding his disfigured form, and prayed with groans and writhings that she might never look on him again. So days went by.

There came a time when, even through his all-absorbing thought of self, there pierced the consciousness that he no longer could impose upon the goat-herds' bounty. Food was scarce within the hut, and even though he groaned to die, the dawns brought hunger. So at the close of day he dragged him down the mountainside, thinking that under cover of the dusk he would steal into the village and seek a chance to earn his bread.

But as he neared the little town and the sound of evening bells broke on his ear, and lighted windows marked the homes where welcome waited other men, he winced as from a blow. This was the village he had thought to enter in the midst of loud acclaims, its brave deliverer from the Province Terror. Then every window in the hamlet would have blazed for him. Then every door would have been set wide to welcome Aldebaran, the royal son of kings, fittest to bear the Sword of Conquest. And now Aldebaran was but the crippled makeshift of a man, who could not even draw that Sword from out its scabbard; at whose wry features all must turn away in loathing, and some perchance might even set the dogs to snarling at his heels, in haste to have him gone.

"In all the world," he cried in bitterness, "there breathes no other man whom Faith hath used so cruelly! Emptied of hope, robbed of my all, life doth become a prison-house that dooms me to its lowest dungeon! Why struggle any longer 'gainst my lot? Why not lie here and starve, and thus force Death to turn the key, and break the manacles which bind me to my misery?"

While he thus mused, footsteps came up the mountainside, a lusty voice was raised in song, and before he could draw back into cover, a head in a fantastic cap appeared above the bushes. It was the village Jester capering along the path as if the world were thistledown and every day a holiday. But when he saw Aldebaran he stopped agape and crossed himself. Then he pushed nearer.

Now those who saw the Jester only on a market day or at the country fair plying his trade of merriment for all 'twas worth knew not a sage was hid behind that motley or that his sympathies were tender as a saint's. Yet so it was. The motto written deep across his heart was this: "*To ease the burden of the world!*" It was beyond belief how wise he'd grown in wheedling men to think no load lay on their shoulders. Now he stood and gazed upon the prostrate man who turned away his face and would not answer his low-spoken words: "What ails thee, brother?"

It boots not in this tale what wiles he used to gain Aldebaran's ear and tongue. Another man most surely must have failed, because he shrank from pity as from salt rubbed in a wound, and felt that none could hear his woeful history and not bestow that pity. But if the Jester felt its throbs he gave no sign. Seated beside him on the grass he talked in the light tone that served his trade, as if Aldebaran's woes were but a flight of swallows 'cross a summer sky, and would as soon be gone. And when between his quirks he'd drawn the piteous tale entirely from him, he doubled up with laughter and smote his sides.

"And I'm the fool and thou'rt the sage!" he gasped between his peals of mirth. "Gadzooks! Methinks it is the other way around. Why, look ye, man! Here thou dost go a-junketing through all the earth to find a chance to show unequalled courage, and when kind Fate doth shove it underneath thy very nose, thou turn'st away, lamenting. I've heard of those who know not beans although the bag be opened, and now I laugh to see one of that very kind before me."

Then dropping his unseemly mirth and all his wanton raillery, he stood up with his face a-shine, and spake as if he were the heaven-sent messenger of hope.

"Rise up!" he cried. "*Knowest thou not it takes a thousandfold more courage to sheathe the sword when one is all on fire for action than to go forth against the greatest foe?* Here is thy chance to show the world the kingliest spirit it has ever known! Here is a phalanx thou mayst meet all single-handed—a daily struggle with a host of hurts that cut thee to the quick. This sheathèd sword upon thy side will stab thee hourly with deeper thrusts than any adversary can give. 'Twill be a daily 'minder of thy thwarted hopes. For foiled ambition is the hydra-headed monster of the Lerna marsh. Two heads will rise for every one thou severest. 'Twill be a fight till death. Art brave enough to lift the gauntlet that Despair flings down and wage this warfare to thy very grave?'"

Such call to arms seemed mockery as Aldebaran looked down upon his twisted limbs, but as the bloodstone on his finger met his sight his kingly soul leapt up. "I'll keep the oath!" he cried, and struggling to his feet laid hand upon the jewelled hilt that decked his side.

"By sheathèd sword, since blade is now denied me," he swore. "I'll win the future that my stars foretold!"

In that exalted moment all things seemed possible, and though his body limped as haltingly he followed on behind his new-found friend, his spirit walked erect, and faced his future for the time, undaunted.

His merry-Andrew of a host made festival when they at last came to his dwelling; lit a great fire upon the hearth, brewed him a drink that warmed him to the core, brought wheaten loaves and set a bit of savoury meat to turning on the spit.

"Ho, ho!" he laughed. "They say it is an ill wind that blows good to none. Now thou dost prove the proverb. The tempest that didst blow thee from thy course mayhap may send me on my way rejoicing. I long have wished to leave this land and seek the distant province where my kindred dwell, but there was never one to take my place. And when I spake of going, my townsmen said me nay. 'Twas quite as bad, they vowed, as if the priest should suddenly desert his parish, with none to shepherd his abandoned flock. 'Who'll cheer us in our doldrums?' they demanded. 'Who'll help us bear our troubles by making us forget them? Thou canst not leave us, Piper, until some other merry soul comes by to set our feet a-dancing.' Now thou art come."

"Yes, *I!* A merry soul indeed!" Aldebaran cried in bitterness.

"Well, maybe not quite that," his host admitted. "But thou couldst pass as one. Thou couldst at least put on my grotesque garb, couldst learn the quips and quirks by which I make men laugh. Thou wouldst not be the first man who has hid an aching heart behind a smile. The tune thou pipest may not bring *thee* pleasure, but if it sets the world to dancing it is enough. And, too, it is an honest way to earn thy bread. Canst think of any other?"

Aldebaran hid his face within his hands. "No, no!" he groaned. "There is no other way, and yet my soul abhors the thought, that I, a king's son, should descend to this! The jester's motley and the cap and bells. How can *I* play such a part?"

"Because thou *art* a king's son," said the Jester. "That in itself is ample reason that thou shouldst play more royally than other men whatever part Fate may assign thee."

Aldebaran sat wrapped in thought. "Well," was the slow reply after long pause, "an hundred years from now, I suppose, 'twill make no difference how circumstances chafe me now. A poor philosophy, but still there is a grain of comfort in it. I'll take thy offer, friend, and give thee gratitude."

And so next day the two went forth together. Aldebaran showed a brave front to the crowd, glad of the painted mask that hid his features, and no one guessed the misery that lurked beneath his laugh, and no one knew what mighty tax it was upon his courage to follow in the Jester's lead and play buffoon upon the open street. It was a thing he loathed, and yet, 'twas as the Jester said, his training in the royal court had made him sharp of wit and quick to read men's minds; and to the countrymen who gathered there agape, around him in the square, his keen replies were wonderful as wizard's magic.

And when he piped—it was no shallow fluting that merely set the rustic feet a-jig, it was a strange and stirring strain that made the simplest one among them stand with his soul a-tiptoe, as he listened, as if a kingly train with banners went a-marching by. So royally he played his part, that even on that first day he surpassed his teacher. The Jester, jubilant that this was so, thought that his time to leave was near at hand, but when that night they reached his dwelling Aldebaran tore off the painted mask and threw himself upon the hearth.

"'Tis more than flesh can well endure!" he cried. "All day the thought of what I've lost was like a constant sword-thrust in my heart. Instead of deference and respect that once was mine from high and low, 'twas laugh and jibe and pointing finger. And, too" (his voice grew shrill and querulous), "I saw young lovers straying in the lanes together. How can I endure that sight day after day when my arms must remain for ever empty? And little children prattled by their father's side no matter where I turned. I, who shall never know a little son's caress, felt like a starving man who looks on bread and may not eat. Far better that I crawl away from haunts of men where I need never be tormented by such contrasts."

The Jester looked down on Aldebaran's wan face. It was as white and drawn as if he had been tortured by the rack and thumbscrew, so he made no answer for the moment. But when the fire was kindled, and they had supped the broth set out in steaming bowls upon the table, he ventured on a word of cheer.

"At any rate," he said, "for one whole day thou hast kept thy oath. No matter what the anguish that it cost thee, from sunrise to sunsetting thou hast held Despair at bay. It was the bravest stand that thou hast ever made. And now, if thou hast lived through this one day, why not another? 'Tis only one hour at a time that thou art called on to endure. Come! By the bloodstone that is thy birthright, pledge me anew thou'lt keep thy oath until the going down of one more sun."

So Aldebaran pledged him one more day, and after that another and another, until a fortnight slowly dragged itself away. And then because he met his hurt so bravely and made no sign, the Jester thought the struggle had grown easier with time, and spoke again of going to his kindred.

"Nay, do not leave me yet," Aldebaran plead. "Wouldst take my only crutch? It is thy cheerful presence that alone upholds me."

"Yet it would show still greater courage if thou couldst face thy fate alone," the Jester answered. "Despair cannot be vanquished till thou hast taught thyself to really feel the gladness thou dost feign. I've heard that if one will count his blessings as the faithful tell their rosary beads he will forget his losses in pondering on his many benefits. Perchance if thou wouldst try that plan it might avail."

So Aldebaran went out determined to be glad in heart as well as speech, if so be it he could find enough of cheer. "I will be glad," he said, "because the morning sun shines warm across my face." He slipped a golden beam upon his memory string.

"I will be glad because that there are diamond sparkles on the grass and larks are singing in the sky." A dew-drop and a bird's trill for his rosary.

"I will be glad for bread, for water from the spring, for eyesight and the power to smell the budding lilacs by the door; for friendly greetings from the villages."

A goodly rosary, symbol of all the things for which he should be glad, was in his hand at close of day. He swung it gaily by the hearth that night, recounting all his blessings till the Jester thought, "At last he's found the cure."

But suddenly Aldebaran flung the rosary from him and hid his face within his hands. "'Twill drive me mad!" he cried. "To go on stringing baubles that do but set my mind the firmer on the priceless jewel I have lost. May heaven forgive me! I am not really glad. 'Tis all a hollow mockery and pretence!"

Then was the Jester at his wit's end for a reply. It was a welcome sound when presently a knocking at the door broke on the painful silence. The visitor who entered was an aged friar beseeching alms at every door, as was the custom of his brotherhood, with which to help the sick and poor. And while the Jester searched within a chest for some old garments he was pleased to give, he bade the friar draw up to the hearth and tarry for their evening meal, which then was well-nigh ready. The friar, glad to accept the hospitality, spread out his lean hands to the blaze, and later, when the three sat down together, warmed into such a cheerfulness of speech that Aldebaran was amazed.

"Surely thy lot is hard, good brother," he said, looking curiously into the wrinkled face. "Humbling thy pride to beg at every door, forswearing thine own good in every way that others may be fed, and yet thy face speaks an inward joy. I pray thee tell me how thou hast found happiness."

"*By never going in its quest,*" the friar answered. "Long years ago I learned a lesson from the stars. Our holy Abbot took me out one night into the quiet cloister, and pointing to the glittering heavens showed me my duty in a way I never have forgot. I had grown restive in my lot and chafed against its narrow round of cell and cloister. But in a word he made me see that if I stepped aside from that appointed path, merely for mine own pleasure, 'twould mar the order of God's universe as surely as if a planet swerved from its eternal course.

"'No shining lot is thine,' he said. 'Yet neither have the stars themselves a light. They but reflect the Central Sun. And so mayst thou, while swinging onward, faithful to thy orbit, reflect the light of heaven upon thy fellow men.'

"Since then I've had no need to go a-seeking happiness, for bearing cheer to others keeps my own heart a-shine.

"I pass the lesson on to thee, good friend. Remember, men need laughter sometimes more than food, and if thou hast no cheer thyself to spare, why, thou mayst go a-gathering it from door to door as I do crusts, and carry it to those who need."

Long after the good friar had supped and gone, Aldebaran sat in silence. Then crossing to the tiny casement that gave upon the street, he stood and gazed up at the stars. Long, long he mused, fitting the friar's lesson to his own soul's need, and when he turned away, the old astrologer's prophecy had taken on new meaning.

"As Aldebaran the star shines in the heavens" (*no light within itself, but borrowing from the Central Sun*), "so Aldebaran the man might shine among his fellows." (*Beggared of joy himself, yet flashing its reflection athwart the lives of others.*)

When next he went into the town he no longer shunned the sights that formerly he'd passed with face averted, for well he knew that if he would shed joy and hope on others he must go to places where they most abound. What matter that the thought of Vesta stabbed him nigh to madness when he looked on hearth-fires that could never blaze for him? With courage almost more than human he put that fond ambition out of mind as if it were another sword he'd learned to sheathe. At first it would not stay in hiding, but flew the scabbard of his will to thrust him sore as often as he put it from him. But after awhile he found a way to bind it fast, and when he'd found that way it gave him victory over all.

A little child came crying towards him in the marketplace, its world a waste of woe because the toy it cherished had been broken in its play. Aldebaran would have turned aside on yesterday to press the barbed thought still deeper in his heart that he had been denied the joy of fatherhood. But now he stooped as gently as if he were the child's own sire to wipe its tears and soothe its sobs. And when with skilful fingers he restored the toy, the child bestowed on him a warm caress out of its boundless store.

He passed on with his pulses strangely stirred. 'Twas but a crumb of love the child had given, yet, as Aldebaran held it in his heart, behold a miracle! It grew full-loaf, and he would fain divide it with all hungering souls! So when a stone's throw farther on he met a man well-nigh distraught from many losses, he did not say in bitterness as once he would have done, that 'twas the common lot of mortals; to look on him if one would know the worst that Fate can do. Nay, rather did he speak so bravely of what might still be wrung from life though one were maimed like he, that hope sprang up within his hearer and sent him on his way with face a-shine.

That grateful smile was like a revelation to Aldebaran, showing him he had indeed the power belonging to the stars. Beggared of joy, no light within himself, yet from the Central Sun could he reflect the hope and cheer that made him as the eye of Taurus 'mong his fellows.

The weeks slipped into months, months into years. The Jester went his way unto his kindred and never once was missed, because Aldebaran more than filled his place. In time the town forgot it ever had another Jester, and in time Aldebaran began to feel the gladness that he only feigned before.

And then it came to pass, whenever he went by, men felt a strange, strength-giving influence radiating from his presence,—a sense of hope. One could not say exactly what it was, it was so fleeting, so intangible, like warmth that circles from a brazier, or perfume that is wafted from an unseen rose.

Thus he came down to death at last, and there was dole in all the Province, so that pilgrims, journeying through that way, asked when they heard his passing-bell, "What king is dead, that all thus do him reverence?"

"'Tis but our Jester," one replied. "A poor maimed creature in his outward seeming, and yet so blithely did he bear his lot, it seemed a kingly spirit dwelt among us, and earth is poorer for his going."

All in his motley, since he'd willed it so, they laid him on his bier to bear him back again unto his father's house. And when they found the Sword of Conquest hidden underneath his mantle, they marvelled he had carried such a treasure with him through the years, all unbeknown even to those who walked the closest at his side.

When, after many days, the funeral train drew through the castle gate, the king came down to meet it. There was no need of blazoned scroll to tell Aldebaran's story. All written in his face it was, and on his scarred and twisted frame; and by the bloodstone on his finger the old king knew his son had failed not in the keeping of his oath. More regal than the royal ermine seemed his motley now. More eloquent the sheathed sword that told of years of inward struggle than if it bore the blood of dragons, for on his face there shone the peace that comes alone of mighty triumph.

The king looked round upon his nobles and his stalwart sons, then back again upon Aldebaran, lying in silent majesty.

"Bring royal purple for the pall," he faltered, "and leave the Sword of Conquest with him! No other hands will ever be found worthier to claim it!"

That night when tall white candles burned about him there stole a white-robed figure to the flower-strewn bier. 'Twas Vesta, decked as for a bridal, her golden tresses falling round her like a veil. They found her kneeling there beside him, her face like his all filled with starry light, and round them both was such a wondrous shining, the watchers drew aside in awe.

"'Tis as the old astrologers foretold," they whispered. "Her soul hath entered on its deathless vigil. In truth he was the bravest that this earth has ever known."

THE END.

Milton Keynes UK
Ingram Content Group UK Ltd.
UKHW030138180324
439604UK00005B/848